Tantric Bliss

Tantric Bliss

WHEN CONSCIOUSNESS ENTERED ENERGY

SHAKTI PADMINI

TANTRIC BLISS
WHEN CONSCIOUSNESS ENTERED ENERGY

iUniverse books may be ordered through booksellers or by contacting:

iUniverse
1663 Liberty Drive
Bloomington, IN 47403
www.iuniverse.com
1-800-Authors (1-800-288-4677)

Because of the dynamic nature of the Internet, any web addresses or links contained in this book may have changed since publication and may no longer be valid. The views expressed in this work are solely those of the author and do not necessarily reflect the views of the publisher, and the publisher hereby disclaims any responsibility for them.

Illustrations: Doyle Saylor (main photography), Danita Easton (photo-assistant), Shakti Padmini (photo edits)
Additional illustrations: Patrick Gagne (Creatrix) Greg Trinka (Due Date), Shakti Padmini (photo edits)

ISBN: 978-1-4917-3748-4 (sc)
ISBN: 978-1-4917-3749-1 (e)

Library of Congress Control Number: 2014910955

Printed in the United States of America.

iUniverse rev. date: 09/30/2014

To My Beloved,
The Light that sustains me
The consciousness I emerge from
The divine flame which
 I throw myself wholeheartedly into
The God of my heart
I love you

PREFACE

"You *have to* write a book!"
	My friends kept poking me...
"You *should* write a book!"
	My students kept suggesting...
"You *need* to write a book!"
	My best friend was urging me...
"Mom, the fairies are telling me you *must* write a book"
My daughter in a sing song voice was announcing...

Who?
	Me?
		I have nothing to say that has not been said yet
"Oh yes, you have." (Who's that voice?)
	Oh no
"Oh yes, yes, you have!"
	Well, maybe in ten years, when I'm more enlightened...
	When I have more time...
			Then She entered:
"You have to publish your poetry!"
	What?
"You are going to publish your poems!"
	But, but some of them are private...not meant to be seen
"You and me are one"
"You no longer live in separation (though at times you do like
to pretend)
And thus you are no longer private..."

But what if people don't like them?

"Who cares?
Those who are already awakened
        Will rejoice with them
Those who are awakening
            Will be inspired
Those who are ready to awaken
            Will awaken through them
And in those yet in a need of awakening
        Something will quietly start budding inside.."
    Okay, I surrender. I will.
    When?
"Now!"

INTRODUCTION

This is *not* an Erotic Poetry book. And if it is, it's as erotic as the breath you take, as luscious as the open petals of a flower, as juicy as a red ripe strawberry, as sensuous as sunset, as seductive as the full moon, and as passionate as ocean waves...It is a book about life. It is a book about the principles that make our magnificent universe, about the energies flowing through our world - our bodies - our beings, about the Beloved everyone seeks: in another, in nature, within one's heart. It's also a workbook. Each poem is charged with energy that reaches 'under' the mind, talking to the higher aspect of your self, consciously aligning you with. Even if you may not always understand the full meaning of the poem the higher self knows. It rejoices, smiles, and dances. And thus your divine magnificence, the great love energy- consciousness that you are, comes forth.

May you pause for a moment as you read my poems: may you dream, read in between the lines and listen to your body, sensing feelings, allowing visions to appear. May you listen to the small voice from deep within, the voice of the one who remembers... the one who remembers the time *when consciousness entered energy...*

The Fable: Return of The Divine Couple

Long, long time ago, when the Earth was sacred, and all its creatures considered our brothers and sisters, when all the streams were crystal clear and the pure air was sparkling with life force, when men and women lived in love, harmony and flowing abundance, that was the time of the Divine Couple: They were two, but they knew they were one. They had two bodies but one beating heart of God. They did not know separation, thus She, the goddess, was recognized and treasured in every woman, the Earth, the Moon and all creation. He, the God, was honored in every man, the Sun and all the mysterious unseen and unmanifested, the silent consciousness permeating everything.

She was continuously revered and worshiped for her life-giving power, her creative energy, nurturing qualities and breathtaking inner beauty that permeated her form. She was deeply treasured as the embodiment of love. He was honored for his crystal clarity vision, his tremendous inner strength, highly respected as the protector and space holder for love to dance in. Her womb was cherished as the source of life, the fountain of great power and wisdom, the mystical center from which all creation was being born. His hold was reliable, and His word was trusted, for He was the embodiment of Truth. It was in His conscious eyes She grew more beautiful; it was in Her loving arms He grew stronger and brighter. Together, they loved and worshiped one another for they knew they were the embodiment of divine principles that supported one another and could not be separated. They were love and light dancing together, their harmonious dance essential for survival and wellbeing of all.

It was their perfect harmony that nourished all. It was their perfect polarity (though perfectly balanced within) that would create sexual attraction, inspiring force for more love, magic and passion for life to flow.

They danced as one when together, and they danced as one even when physically separated, sensing within the presence of the other. She would feel his still light penetrating her body, holding her safe, radiant and strong in her feminine softness. He would feel the nourishment of Her love, Her ecstatic presence in His heart. Being complete within they were free to give fully and selflessly to one another, and to the community, who they felt a part of their larger body: there were simply no others.

Out of the passionate, ecstatic, blissful union of the divine couple life on Earth flourished.

Gaia, the Earth Herself, was tingling with ecstasy and radiance. She felt being held, being well taken care of, and the fruit of her love emanated from her womb as an abundance of beauty, sparkling waters and food for everyone....

What happened?

Where did it go?

What happened to our Earth?

Why is She crying?

Where did the Divine Couple disappear?

Was it an evolution of the human mind that forgot about the body?

Was it the growth of the intellect that forgot about the heart?

Or was it only a part of the cycle, the great cosmic game, where nothing remains the same?

The veil fell in, the goddess got forgotten, the man got lost.

Separate from love, he did not know his way.

Separated from love, separate from all creation.

Separate even from his other forms of human embodiment.

He knew he was looking for something, he thought it was power that he would find on the outside. He wanted to prove himself, to be more powerful than "others". In his search for power he destroyed.

She cried. She called, but without His powerful light shining inside her, her voice was not heard. Without His reverent holding, she lost her radiance. Her sinuous dance became erratic. Separate from him, she became just an energy, energy that he, in his ignorance feared.

In order to survive in the world he dominated, she took on some of his ways, suppressing her tender essence. His light weakened, his authentic power diminished. In his search for his lost inner power (that of course cannot be found on the outside), he nearly destroyed the planet.

If only he looked down into his heart that was crying empty, if only he felt his body, that was yearning to be held in love's arms.

In the meantime, She was imprisoned in an armor of anger, sulking for what he has done to her, for what he has done to her Earth. Missing his conscious sight, she did not feel beautiful. In her strive to be seen once more, she put much effort in trying to enhance her external beauty, reshaping her body this way and that (also forgetting her true beauty comes from within). If only she could fully feel her pain (the pain of the world), in her tears dissolve the protection of her heart.

Both lost and confused, they try to distract themselves from their pain with entertainment, striving to fill that empty space with power, sex, money or objects they can buy, but sooner or later the pangs return...

Lost and confused they wander aimlessly, searching for elusive happiness, unconsciously searching for love and light, their true essence, for each other, unaware of that they are looking for lies deep inside them, hidden underneath layers of lies.

The wheel of evolution has spun a full cycle. We are ready to begin a new loop of a spiral. The time has come to awaken from this unconscious game, for She, mother Gaia, has had enough. She may have got hurt, but She has never lost her power: She can shiver, She can shake, She can spit out hot lava or move the oceans, sweep all Her creation back deep inside her womb and start all over again...But is that the New Beginning we have in mind? Or can we just resurrect the Divine Couple once more? Can she become She, the embodiment of love, with an open heart and creative womb, can he become He, the mighty, strong, steady presence overseeing the ever changing world, holding space for love and transformation to dance in? Can their passion for another give rise to compassion for all? Can they unite in harmony so new life emerges out of her desperately waiting, pregnant womb?

I say YES we can. We are all divine beings with God's blueprint in our DNA and endless potential. We can re-create this world to our image, make it a cutting edge of evolution where LOVE (not pain) is the evolutionary force, where PASSION and JOY are driving forces to make things happen. We can turn this planet into a blindingly radiant, beautiful jewel of our galaxy, and exquisite living library of billions of life forms.

Resurrecting the Divine Couple is the true purpose of Tantra, whether we talk about physical relationship or inner energetic balance. It is where oneness is found, it is where God (or whatever name you have for that awesome intelligence that's behind all creation) resides. Seemingly small steps you take in your own transformation affect the whole in a big way! Take a leap and begin to live the real lover-beloved romance, discover how much beauty and magic it holds....

THE SECRETS OF TANTRA

Tantra is a timeless path of spiritual (God) realization, embracing life in it's fullness and completeness, recognizing sacredness and divinity in all forms, light and dark equally as one. Though ancient India has given Tantra its Sanskrit name: **Tanoti** = to expand (one's awareness), **Trayati** = to liberate (oneself from the limitations of ego), it has existed in all cultures throughout the ages that worshipped the feminine principle, nurturing close connection with nature and earth. Many books have been written on the subject of Tantra, yet only a few may have captured the grand picture of it, beyond set of sexual practices and exercises.

Tantra is a way of seeing, perceiving and understanding life: the whole universe is Tantric, from the tiny particles in the atom to the great galaxies. In Tantric eyes the all pervading consciousness beyond everything is the (divine) masculine principle, known as Shiva or He. The whole world we live in has been spun into form by (divine) feminine principle, Shakti, or She. She is the energy of creation that in our body we call sexual energy. It is the magical sexual union of those two inseparable cosmic principles that makes life possible. Tantra is inherently embodied within us, whether we consciously pursue it or not, it is simply how we are made. This innate makeup is a key of bringing us back to the source, realizing our infinite, eternal divine nature.

It is She, the divine feminine that has given a men his body. It is He, the divine masculine that gives woman her conscious awareness. Driven together by force sexual attraction He and She are never apart. It is the union of consciousness and energy that makes love happen.

Spirit and Sex cannot be separated. Love arising from (sexual) union of He and She is the fabric that holds this universe together. Let's celebrate love as our innermost essence!

CONTENTS

WELCOME HOME

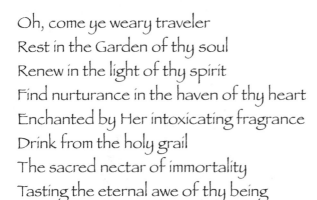

Oh, come ye weary traveler
Rest in the Garden of thy soul
Renew in the light of thy spirit
Find nurturance in the haven of thy heart
Enchanted by Her intoxicating fragrance
Drink from the holy grail
The sacred nectar of immortality
Tasting the eternal awe of thy being

From Her womb you have emerged
And to Her womb you shall return
Your life is a gracious gift of She
Her love unbounded and unconditional
She dwells within and without
In the infinite walls of your heart

Oh, come ye weary traveler
Step over the threshold
And let the magic of your being flow
Now is the time
Go on

I AM

Who am I?

I am a ray of sunshine

in a droplet of the morning dew

I am a rainbow

the evening sky

in all shades of pink and blue

I am a speck of light

I am many specks of light

I am a white bird on his heavenly flight

I am a dream

I am a dreamer

The great creator of my world

I am the great void

Into which all goes back

A matrix

from which all unfolds

I am the breath

I am a wave

The eternal pulsation of the universe

I am the Goddess dancing in the ecstasy

the passionate dance of creation

I am the marriage of Shakti and Shiva

in the etheric Temple of the Heart

I am a speck of light

I am many, *many* specks of light

I am the sound of Om

Consciousness turning into matter

I am pure LOVE

naked

I am sex energy transformed

An infinite ocean of bliss

I am eternity

I am Divinity

I am nothing

I am everything

I am.....You

TANTRA

She magnetized him with her sweet sensuality

He electrified her with his luminous presence

They got lost in one another

Riding the wave of orgasmic bliss

As their hearts merged, they disappeared into light

Only pure love remained...

SPRING MAGIC

Oh beloved,
Let me welcome your seed in my sacred garden
So I can sprout a precious flower bud
Oh beloved,
Let me shine my beam of light
So your precious flower blossoms
Releasing the fragrance of love
Together we get intoxicated
Divinely drunk
We'll melt in the sweetness

of the holy nectar...

BLOSSOMING

My radiant one,

Nurtured by the warmth of your ever present light

I blossom into a beautiful flower of love

My blossoming one,

Flooded by your intoxicating fragrance

I dissolve myself in you

Love is what IS

Love's what's ever been

A blossom filled with magic

So pure, sweet and clean

A sunlight captured in a form

To be tasted, smelled and seen

Filled with divine nectar

The liquid taste of bliss

Love is what has ever been

Love is all there *is*

FLOWER CALL

My dearest Shiva sunshine

Stay with me

Shine into me

Open me

Fill me with your love

Until I can contain myself no more

My dearest Shakti love

Receive me

Receive me

Open the petals of your heart

Bathe me in your ecstasy

Until I dissolve in you

AUTUMN SEDUCTION

Luscious Autumn flower
Reaching up to the sky
See me! Feel me!
She calls to the Sun up high
He rejoices in Her beauty
Embracing Her in His warmest beams
Held by the stillness of His loving light
Radiant love She streams
As He merges into Her
(Expressed in Her fragrant glow)
New universe is being born
New seeds of Love begin to grow

HOLY NIGHT

My Beloved,
Like a million stars you are shining bright
Penetrating me with thy light
My Beloved,
I am losing myself in you
As in the velvet sky of holy night
Into the depths of your galactic womb
You're receiving me
And so we merge in cosmic flight
Dissolving in divine light

COSMIC GAME

In your eyes I see the fire

That ignites true love's desire

In your eyes I see the ocean

That sets creation in motion

Fire makes the waters boiling

Goddess Kundalini uncoiling

Mighty gods and devas dance

Enchanted in divine trance

Ignorance does not have a chance

The fires burn...

Sex into Love, lust into passion

Hearts melt in endless compassion

Shakti back to Shiva

Shiva back to cosmic void

Love that nothing can't avoid

That nothing which from everything came

That's the greatest cosmic game

PLAYING NAMES

And the poet
With her gentle heart
She saw it all
She saw
How she played her part
She saw beyond faces
Beyond ego
Beyond gender
She saw
That there was only love
Sweet and tender
She saw
That dark and light are the same
The same cosmic energy that came
Out of the nothingness of void
Out of that great beyond the beyond
And if you look upside down
Dark turns into light
And if you stand on Earth
Day spins into a night
And the moon
Reflects the sun's shine
In such delight
And only out of darkness
Born is a star shining bright

So sleep my child
For when morning comes
Love illuminates all
And we will laugh
How we got caught
In playing names

TANTRIC BLISS

When consciousness entered energy

Love was born

As they kept on making love the whole universe came into being

She danced, swirled, undulated, being held in his arms

She spun light into matter and gave birth to stars

He kept on holding, relentlessly penetrating Her

While She shapeshifted, flowing form to form

When consciousness entered energy I was there

Drunk with bliss, dizzy with infinity

Boundless being of boundless love

In tears with gratitude and awe

And I gave promise to live that love

To live that bliss

In every dewdrop, in petals of a rose

In every soft kiss

Remember? Remember?

I am here,

I am that love

I am that union of the Earth below

And the sky above

I am the open yoni

Holding the shaft of light

I am the lover and beloved

Him and Her

Marriage of day and night

When consciousness entered energy

The sacred life begun

And goes on

HER YEARNING

Love me, my beloved,

Love me, take all of me

Take me all, don't leave anything out

Take my shadow

Take my light

Take my laughter

Take my tears

Take my anger

Take my Love

Hold me, hold me tight

Kiss my lips

Until they melt into a sweet honey

To sweeten your breath of life

Kiss my breasts

Until they feed you full with nectar of love

Kiss my belly

To awaken the Cosmic Womb

Womb Divine mother

Your home

Kiss my yoni

Until my body dissolves in you stillness

Until with a soft cry

She opens all her petals

To reveal the diamond in the center

The center of my heart

The center of my soul

A complete surrender to You-God

Then

Let your mighty Wand of Light

Destroy all the illusion there's ever been

The illusion of two

Let there be only one

One mind

One body

One soul

One being of love

One eternity

One

ENCOUNTER

Our eyes met

Our lips touched

Our hearts leapt

Our bodies came together

We made love

We merged

I fell asleep with you inside me

I woke up with you inside me

I move through my day with you still inside me!

I am a walking universe

I am so wide, wider than you can see!

Oh beloved, what have you done?

I giggle.....

MOTHER EARTH

She pulses
She breathes
She feels
She creates
She gives birth
She gives
She nurtures
She cares
She loves
She's love

> My heart pulses
> I breathe
> I give birth
> I give
> I nurture
> I care
> I love
> I am love ~ I am She

She's been hurt
> And yet She still smiles

She's been exploited
> And yet She still blossoms

She's been violated
> And yet She still loves

She's been taken
> And yet She still gives

And so can I
> For love can never
>> be broken

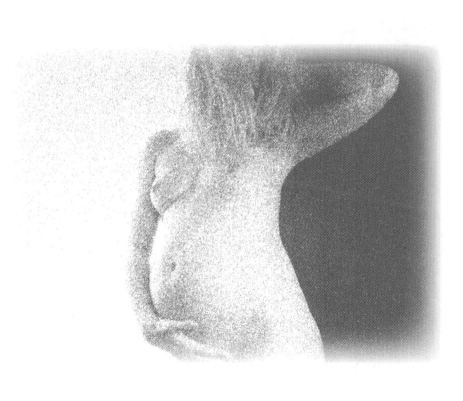

CREATRIX

———❦———

I am the great Creatrix
Frisky with sacred energy
Spiraling inside my womb
Delirious with desire
Longing with lust for life
Yearning to give birth to my love
I dance
 I sway
I swirl
Undulate in ecstasy
I am the feminine in heat
Wild
Unstoppable
My sacred peach ripe and swollen
Her luscious lips dripping with sweet nectar
My nipples tingle in the radiance of my heart
As I spin void into light
                As I spin light into beauty
As I make consciousness manifest in being

THE DARK FEMININE

As the New Moon rises
My womb sheds all her creation
I am her
I am dark Luna
My blood and tears
Wash away all the past
All that is no more
I am death
I am blackness
Deep
All consuming
Terrifying
Love in disguise
Do not talk to me!
Do not engage my mind!
For I have no mind
Instead
Listen to the voice
From the deep
Do not be swayed by my emotions!
They are the waves of the oceans
Washing over you
Grinding you to the steady core
But hold me tight
Feel the beat of my heart

Do not look into my eyes
For they are filled with rage
Bolts of lightning to stun you
But see me inside out
Make Love to me
Take me in my death
Enter my blackness
Pierce my dark heart
With your light
The heart that's been crying for your love
Do not be afraid of my power
Do not ask
Just do it
Now!

YONI

Secret garden
Sacred temple
Portal to heavenly bliss
Holy gate to universal mystery
Holy as holiness can be
Gateway to the cosmic womb
The womb of divine mother
Venerable shrine of She
Guardian of the lotus heart
Only pure love and devotion is the key
Soft, tender and delicate
Vulnerable in her sensitivity
Yet holding so much power
the power of creativity
the power of divinity
the power of the goddess
Do not come near without bringing offerings
Do not approach without bowing deep
Surrender
Wish to take nothing
And give everything
She is to be worshiped by thousand prostrations
Adored by precious jewels and beautiful flowers
Caressed by thousand gentle strokes
Loved by thousand tender kisses

Only the pure in heart may enter
Only pure wand of holy light may illuminate
Beaming in selfless luminosity
Giving himself fully
Willing to give all
Willing to die for the goddess
Only then she shares her secret
The divine nectar
A priceless gift
Worth dying for

THE DARK ONE

She is dark
She is fierce
She is passionately wild
And frighteningly powerful
But you mustn't show your fear
She's the dark seductress
Sexual energy in raw form
Awaiting transformation
And you must not run away
She is the opposite side of the coin
The shadow of the virgin
Guardian of the innocent one
You must not turn away
She's the testing force of your light
She's the lightning storm to your stillness
Will you stand tall and straight?
Will you shine in your light?
She'll try to pull you down in her blackness
The murky, treacherous waters
If you drop down
Into lust
Or react with emotion
You'll drawn
Love will be lost
If you reject her

Love will remain imprisoned
If you fear her
She'll destroy you
There's only one way:
Shine, shine, shine!
And love her, love her, love her!
Love her in her blackness
Love her in her dark passion
Recognize her fierce beauty
Dance with her
Until she surrenders to you
See right through her disguise
Into her tender, loving heart

DREAMING

Last night I had a dream: I took a form

I had this thing called a body

With arms and legs that appeared solid

Pulsing with blood that was warm

I lived on a small planet

Also made of light

Weaved into beauty so real

To feed my sensual delight

Learned how to touch

And taste

And smell

And feel

Lost in my play

Wrapped in the veil of forgetting

But it was not too tight

As with time it began to peel

I yearned for wings so I could fly

Free as a bird in the wide blue sky

I knew I could do it - if only if I could let go

Of that troublesome mind

that kept saying NO

And sometimes I'd just do it

I'd soar high

Then fall on my face

Beat and bruised

Naked in disgrace

In the middle of night (still within a dream)

I'd cry to God: I'm done

Please take me home!

And the voice inside replied

You are here

There's nowhere to go

Can you hear my OM?

I'd take a deep breath

Kept walking on the winding trail

Rising and falling

Peeking through and

Getting tangled in the veil

Then one day

When looking into God's eyes

Past merged into present

Future swallowed the past

And The Earth kissed the sky

I woke up from my dream

My body swallowed the universe

That burst inside me

Into the eternal I

Drowned in the ocean of love

The sweetest death that can ever be

Born into which never dies

Beloved, I am Thee!

Please hold me, my dearest

When I start drifting into dreams

Pinch me if I fall slumbering too deep

This world is spinning

As far as I'm dreaming

But when I wake up

Beyond the stars we'll leap!

TO BE BEHELD

Hey stranger
Stop running!
I know who you are!
Stop hiding
I know where your dwelling is
Stop moving around in circles
Make an A-line
For you are an arrow
Pointed directly to pierce my heart
I no longer resist the impact
Hey stranger!
Stop hanging your head low
Show me your face!
The face I've always known
I've seen it in a mirror
As long as I can remember
Yearning to touch it
Yearning to be touched
I walked the narrow winding trail
Until I came to a wall
I tried to fight it with fists
Until my knuckles got raw
But it did not budge
In fact - the more I fought it
Stronger it grew it seems

Now, when my physical strength is exhausted
My only way is down
Down on my knees
Down to become the earth
That holds the wall

Earth

The chalice of love

BELOVED

Beloved,

You came for me...
Finding me raw and vulnerable
In my deep longing for you
 Taken aback a little by your actual presence
Yearning to fully give myself to you

And afraid a little of being taken
Wanting to take the leap
And scrambling for roots to hold on
When the ground begins to shake

I've given you million puzzles
Put you through million tests
Made you walk through the fire
Just to know that you are real

And perhaps there will be million more

Coming from the dark unconscious of my womb

But in the light of my heart

I *see you*

You are my prince charming

Willing to slay a twelve-
  headed dragon

Just to hold my hand

You are the brightest white flame

Burning through all illusion

Passionately consuming all

And I in deep surrender

Yearn to be eaten by you

Until only purest love remains

 When the sun's in the sky

I knew you were in me

But in the grayness of the fog

I would doubt

And so you showed me

In the dark of the night
You popped right out of my heart

Piercing me with your infinite eyes

To shatter the dream of separation

The little mind still wobbles

My body aches for your form

But the heart knows

We are together

Forever

Dancing in bliss

Swirling with the galaxies

Making infinite love

And giving birth to stars

Beloved within love

Two lovers

Beating as

One heart of God

I love *Thee*!

DEATH

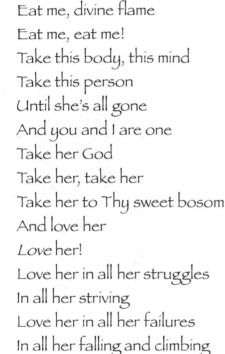

Eat me, divine flame
Eat me, eat me!
Take this body, this mind
Take this person
Until she's all gone
And you and I are one
Take her God
Take her, take her
Take her to Thy sweet bosom
And love her
Love her!
Love her in all her struggles
In all her striving
Love her in all her failures
In all her falling and climbing
She's served well
And now she's tired
Surrendered to your will
She's ready to go
To merge into divine flow
So let her die in your lap
Let her dissolve into flowers
And when she's gone
When she's Thine
You and I are One

MORNING INTERLUDE

God, may I sit next to you at sunrise?
Serenaded by morning birds, singing me into sweet surrender
Being stripped naked by the vibrant, life force dense air
Caressed all over by horizon's rainbow colors
And then....softly kissed by first rays of sun
Oh, how divinely aroused I feel!
My yoni swollen in anticipation
My womb quietly waiting
And when piercing sun enters me in His fullness
I vibrate in ecstasy
My heart overflowing with uncontainable joy
I burst out in a climax like a supernova!
In specks of stardust I inhabit all the beauty of the world...

SILENT

When my eyes look eye to eye to the divine I
I'm silent
When the stillness of my mind
finds words hard to find
I'm silent
When the beating of my heart
Beats in the rhythm of God's art
I'm silent
When the aching of my heart
Exposes all of me
 Raw
Naked
Tears all what I'm not apart
I'm silent
When ecstasy of my body
has the limits of no body
I am silent
When my spirit wants to run wild
jump and tumble like a child
I'm silent
When the bliss of my being
feels without touching
sees without seeing
I am silent
Oh my, oh my, who am I?

I'm silence that speaks louder than words

I'm bliss beyond all appearances

I'm love beyond all creation

In gratitude of embodiment

THE CREATRIX II

I am the great Creatrix
Divine mother in her fertile cycle
Flowing with desire to give life
Filled with relentless passion
Vibrating with love frequency
Higher
    And higher
        And higher
In eternal ecstasy
In a blissful orgasmic tsunami wave
The universe floats out of my womb
And with each contraction of my holy temple
A star is being born
With each sway of my soft, round hips
A light filled galaxy spirals out
Like this one
Filled with so much brightness: Let's call in the Milky way!
Here
A little sweet planet is just being born
I breathe life into her
And make her luminous blue
Just like the waters of my flowing desire
The waters of life
I'll call her the Earth
Contained within hearth: home

She'll be goddess like me
A mother in a form
With a round pregnant belly
Out of which millions of life forms will be born
Two most important ones
One – a *womban* – created in the image of my being
The other – a man – her companion –
Pure consciousness dressed in a body
Encoded within them
Is the divine puzzle
How one can become many
How two can become one
When the puzzle is solved
When the task is done
They will come home
Resting in pure love
In the stillness of my womb

PLAYING WITH GOD

God, may I play with you?

We can play hide and seek:
Oh, how many times you've fooled me!
Hiding in places where I would not dare to look

We can dance:
When you lead
We flow so elegantly
My dress swirls in perfection
My hair blows in the wind
And you never step on my toes
When I lead
We may lose the rhythm
Get tangled up
Bump into each other
Even fall to the ground
Oh my, oh my!

We can dance:
Move back and forth
From formlessness to form
Shape shift from one thing to another
Forget and remember
And forget again
And suddenly remember in the depths of not knowing

We can flirt:

You follow me
And I resist (to test you)
You look into my eyes
With confidence
And I let down my guard
You woo me
And I begin to open
You open your arms
And I let you hold me

We can wrestle:
I wiggle and squiggle
And make lot of fuss
And you just keep your hold
I shout and scream and stomp my feet
And you just smile
And won't let go
I spit fire
And you catch it and turn it into fireworks
You woe me steadily
Relentlessly
And I open more and more
Knowing resistance is futile
You claim me
And I surrender

We can make love:
You touch me
And I soften
You kiss me
And I melt in your arms
You enter me
And I become yours

HIS RESURRECTION

Hey Man!
Get up and stand tall
Jump on your horse
And shine your light
Shoo away the goblins of doubt
Claim your supreme power
Trust in your majestic masculine might

Hey Man!
Go and ride tall
Don't let your own monsters make you small
Claim your princess
Slay the dragons of her pain
Bravely pull her out of the dark cave
And fill her with joy
Don't leave her waiting womb in vain
Cut through the bribes of anger
Surrounding her vulnerable heart
Holding her steadily
Let her know you've never been apart
Holding her firmly yet tenderly
Through all the vicious storms
                            Let them pass
Remaining in the solid core of love
                            Make it last

Hey Man!
Open your arms really wide
And hold Her in all Her forms
With confident, humble pride
Hold the space in which magic happens
Where love and truth are the only weapons
Hold the torch of a guardian of life
Protector of all that's sacred
For place of beauty where happiness will thrive
And compassion blooms without hatred
Hold your mama in her fertile dance
See Her glow in abundance
Steady in your conscious stance
Give peace on Earth another chance
        Give bliss on Earth a newborn chance

Make l o v e: have your goddess glow in radiance!

FALLING

I'm falling
Into the abyss unknown
Swept by a wind unblown
Spreading my arms
Touching nothing
Feeling everything
Finding nothing to hold on

I'm falling
Moved by a force unknown
Leaving behind all that I own
Leaving behind all that I do not own
Losing my self
Finding myself
Finding my being
Becoming my own

I'm falling
Into the depth of my womb
Scared of Her openness
Scared of Her spaciousness
Within the dark of my ego's tomb

I'm falling
Into the sweetness of Her heart
She and I - never apart

WAVES

She's a liquid love:
Once you open she pours into every crevice of your being!
And she moves in waves.

Waves, waves, awesome waves
Never beginning, ending
Rolling, foaming, crashing
Waving, bouncing, crashing
Emerging from endless ocean,
Waves of bliss in constant motion
Come and dive if you dare
In sweet surrender drown your fear
Waves of love to swallow you
Waves of life to inspire you
Waves of love that you can give
Waves of life that you can live
Waves of love within God's heart
Waves of life – the sacred art
Waves of Love: that's what you are!

CREATRIX III

I am She
The great Creatrix
Shaping light into beauty
Giving birth to all things green
You can smell my soul
In the scent of a plant
You can taste my love
In a sweet Amrita of a flower
You can feel my healing embrace
In the stems and branches
Waving in a breeze
My loving arms
Extend like tentacles
To touch your body
To stroke your spirit
Embracing you
Caressing you into awakening
So you can see
How beautiful you are!

NO END

Inside the Great Mother
The dream of life slithers and sways
Carried by waves of love
Within the worldly maze

There's no end
No beginning
As long as She's dreaming
Life goes on
The universe keeps spinning.....

Enjoy the ride
Have a happy dreaming!

EPILOG

Many female Tantra teachers seem to choose not to have children, perhaps in order to focus more fully on their blessed work and Tantric explorations, perhaps to serve humanity more fully with higher purpose without earthen 'distractions'...but is not Tantra very much grounded in the *earth*?

For me, this was not an option! I'd always known I was meant to have children. I was to descend down to the Earth fully and completely, to embody Her entirely, in the radiant splendor and in her mud and blood and messy hair. I wanted to feel the subtle magic conception - two cells merging into one, spirit and sex creating life. I wanted to feel the pulsation of life in my womb. I wanted to drop this self concerned person aside and fully embody Divine Mother to orgasmically usher a new soul into this world. I yearned to feel the flow of my essence - mother's milk - liquid love - into my baby's mouth. I wanted to feel the bliss of my precious little one falling asleep in my arms...I wanted to experience *all* of motherhood, the highs and the lows, the surrender arising from ongoing sleep deprivation that breaks down the rational mind and awakens the dream mind to perceive beyond the veil....I wanted to taste the heart opening joy of endless giving that completely shatters the ego and effaces the person that used to be, and re-creates someone called Mother - someone immensely vulnerable yet strong in her vulnerability, someone who's heart always aches with unconditional love and concern at the thought of her child, who's giving never feels enough... Is it not what the Divine Mother feels for all Her creation? - *That* to me *is* Tantra, oh what an amazing dimension I would have missed out!

However, being on a Tantric path nothing seems simple or easy or straightforward (at least until one fully surrenders) and so my journey to motherhood took twists and turns: Before I could be initiated into giving life I was to be initiated into death: My firstborn was stillborn. His heart stopped beating a few hours into labor. His spirit, however, has never left. And this poem I wrote to him:

DUE DATE

Today, I thought

...I may push you out into my world

Today, I hoped...

I would hold you in my arms

Today I imagined

...Would be the happiest time in my life

But instead

I've got empty arms

I can ask million times

Why?

Why your sweet spirit needed to fly

Why I had to say so quickly

Goodbye?

There's so much pain and sorrow in my heart

But there's also so much love & bliss from what you've given me

There's so much loneliness in my life

But there's also so much light

When I feel your radiant presence

Around me

Memories of you in my belly

Bring so much sweetness

So much joy

Feeling you with me now

Gives me strength

Strength to know

That my love is stronger

Than my sorrow

That my joy is stronger

Than my pain

Thank you for being

Thank you for your sweet Divine presence

Thank you for all that joy!

You will always dwell in my heart

I'm your mama

And you 'll always be

My little boy!

I love you

Forever.....

————————•● June 2001 ●•————————

I've realized that this little man called Adam was indeed the man who initiated me into Tantric union more deeply than anyone else could do: Created in my womb, and out of His love and devotion He never really left it - for I am the Divine Mother and inside my womb He forever dwells.

Thank you, Adam, for awakening my awareness beyond my physical form into who I truly am.

Perhaps the most important knowingness in Tantra is that bliss is always: It resides equally in the heights of divine ecstasy and it the abyss of an intense pain. And where there is bliss, there is love. For when *consciousness* enters *energy*, *l o v e* is born....

Acknowledgments

This book has not been born overnight. Just like a seed laying in the cool earth over chilly winter months, activating its life-force potential through the experience of frost and then germinating underground until eventually its first shoot appears in the daylight, and then continuing to grow over a length of time until finally reaching the magnificent form of a mature plant, I realize there have been influences in my life that has collectively nudged to form that which emerged.

Here I will name only a few, although there have been many, names of some I've never got to know. Gratitude to my parents, grandparents, and my sister, who have co-created the perfect circumstances in which I grew up. To Narayani, my first and the most influential yoga teacher, whose God-sparkles in her eyes were enticing and magnetic, that 'I want those too!' To Sunyata Saraswati and Bodhi Avinasha, whose book 'Jewel in The Lotus' made me jump with excitement feeling I found what I had been searching all my life, and for face to face (Ipsalu) Tantra guidance that followed, to Bernie Prior and his communication of self-realized truth about man and woman that I deeply rejoiced with as the truth of my heart, and his introduction of The-Form - Reality Practice that further deepened my understanding of love, God, consciousness and cosmos, and even myself... To my dearest friends Diana & Richard Kaiser, whose love and continuing selfless giving and caring has made God alive and present even at times when I was swimming in the dark, to all my lovers and mates who pushed me deeper into letting go of who I was not, and to all my students who taught me so much.

To Doyle Saylor and Danita Easton who's enthusiasm to do photo-illustrations as I wished tickled my heart. To my children, Parvati & Danelle, who have been my biggest teachers ever and to my husband, Terry Lightfoot, my Beloved manifest in a form, who's presence, unconditional love and devotion continue to illuminate my being and birth me as love.

My poems reflect the ongoing realizations of a greater reality emerging from my Tantra practice, a truth so loud and magnificent that cannot be ignored anymore. There's a yearning of the Divine Being within each of us to be recognized, fully seen, live, breathe, walk, make love and play and thus allowed to emerge into complete embodiment; to create a new realm of living in love and light, in truth and harmony, to bring Heaven down to Earth. Ascension really is a descension, for when spirit consciousness fully descends in a matter, spirit and matter cease to be separate. That is the Tantric union.

ABOUT THE POET

Rev Shakti Padmini is a certified International Yoga Teacher, certified Ipsalu Tantra Teacher & Healer, founder of Pinklotuss Tantra, teacher of the Sacred Flow Practice (the ultimate dance of Shakti and Shiva, consciousness into embodiment), Ordained Priestess of Isis Temple, Sacred Dancer, (Tantric) doula, poet, writer, artist, natural healer and a devoted, passionate mother. She lives with her partner and two magical children in Northern California.

Recognizing sexual energy as a sacred portal to the Divine, through her *Tantric Work of Many Forms* Shakti has been committed to opening the doors to divinity to others. Her passion is in returning sexual energy to her home in the heart, resurrecting true light of a man and real beauty of a woman - returning the holy communion of God-Goddess once again to the Earth as the supreme act of healing our planet & raising global awareness onto a higher stage of evolution.

Shakti's mission is to bring you the purest form of Tantra: Where sexual energy is not an object of self-gratification, but a sacred vessel that touches the soul; a precious tool for healing, transformation and illumination, a luminous holy grail of unconditional love.

Find out more about **Tantra** and Shakti's mission: www.pinklotuss.com, www.sacrednectar.net, & www.pinklotusherbs.com

Look out for her next, soon to be available book **"My Sacred Journey Through a Messy Life: Tantra as You May** *(not)* **Know It"**, a fascinating a deep dive into living a life in the Tantric paradigm.